YOU CAN OVERCOME THAT ADDICTION

ANTHONY EKANEM

Made with ♥ on the Notion Press Platform
www.notionpress.com

Contents

Preface   v

1. What Is Addiction?   1

2. The Addiction Cycle   3

3. Why People Fail At Overcoming Addiction   5

4. Make A Commitment To Quit   7

5. The Pros And Cons Of Addiction   9

6. Identify Your Triggers   11

7. Make A Quitting Plan   13

8. Prepare Your Environment   15

9. Seek Professional Help   17

10. Surround Yourself With Support   19

11. Handling Withdrawal Symptoms   21

12. Celebrate Your Success   23

13. Track Your Progress   25

Preface

When you are suffering from an addiction, it can feel like your entire life is out of control and you have no power to overcome it. When you are addicted to something, it can also feel like you're completely alone and have nowhere to turn. These are all common mindsets for someone who has an addiction to any substance, whether that is food, cigarettes or other tobacco products, alcohol, prescription, or illegal drugs or even sex. But neither are you alone in your addiction nor do you have to be a slave to addiction for the rest of your life. That's exactly why this book exists.

It is very easy to feel like you are the only one who is experiencing your particular addiction – or the level of addiction you're experiencing – but the truth is, millions of other people experience the same thing you are suffering from. That's because addiction affects more than 10% of the United States population. That means if you were to get on a typical city bus there are probably two or three people on that bus – besides you – that are suffering from some kind of addiction. Don't fool yourself either; having a food addiction or being unable to quit drinking alcohol is the same as an addiction to a drug or any other substance. Addiction is addiction, no matter what the substances.

You Can Beat Addiction If You Try

You have probably heard this in some form or another before and you probably don't believe a word of it. That's because you know that in the past you have tried to get over your addiction yourself and have failed – and you know that it was a sincere effort and that you were doing your best. No one here is disputing that. But what you need to understand is that every single person who has ever been addicted to anything – in the entire world, throughout thousands of years of human history – has had to make an effort several times – sometimes thousands of times – before they finally succeeded. Just because you have tried in the past and haven't succeeded doesn't mean that your future efforts are doomed to failure. The more times you tried in the past, the better the chances are that you will be successful this time.

Don't Lose Hope

Use the tools in this book to give yourself another chance to get over the addiction that is affecting your life. You are in a minor percentage of people who are trying to get help with their addiction. Although 1 out of every 10 people is addicted to something, less than 10% of those addicts try to seek treatment. You want to succeed and that makes a great deal of difference.

CHAPTER ONE

What is Addiction?

In this chapter, we are going to explore exactly what addiction is and why it is so powerful that it has gripped 1 out of every 10 people (in the United States). We will discuss some of the causes of addiction and how the experts are defining it based on the symptoms. This is useful for anyone who has wondered whether they are addicted to a particular habit and where the line is drawn to define someone as an addict.

The Definition of Addiction

What you need to understand about addiction is that the word has several different definitions. For example, physical addiction is the actual physiological sensations that your body has when you don't have the substance that it is addicted to. Let's take cigarettes for example; if someone is addicted to the nicotine in cigarettes and has been smoking for any length of time, quitting will cause them to experience physiological sensations like irritability, a desire to eat, jitteriness and most of all, a need for nicotine.

But addiction is also used as a measurement of how much tolerance the body has built up against a particular substance and an even further form of physical addiction is the difficulty of an addict to resist the temptation when they receive cues – such as a smoker, even years after they quit, having the urge to smoke because they smelled someone else's cigarette.

Psychological Addiction

Psychological addiction is a little bit more complicated. Psychological addiction can best be defined as the need to fill a hole in someone's life or to make up for something else. Emotional addiction happens whether or not a person has a physical addiction, and in fact, people will often switch from one addiction to another because they are trying to solve an emotional problem with something that just doesn't fill it.

The Bottom Line

The bottom line here is that there are no easy definitions for addiction. If you have a fair idea of what addiction is by reading the information in this chapter you will be on the same page as most of the psychologists and experts on addiction that are out there, giving things definitions.

To put it in the simplest terms possible, addiction is the physical desire to partake in addictive behaviour and the physiological factors that come with it such as withdrawal symptoms and tolerance or the emotional state where you need to take part in addictive behaviour to fill some emotional need.

As you go through this book you will learn more about addiction and you may have a much more personal (and perhaps more accurate) definition afterwards.

The Addiction Cycle

If you have ever sought treatment for your addiction, or even read alcoholism or substance abuse guides on the subject, you might have heard of the addiction cycle. This addiction cycle applies to every type of addiction, not just alcoholism or drug abuse, and breaking this cycle – or understanding how to break the cycle once you get into it – can be the key to overcoming your addiction for good. We will explore exactly how the addiction cycle works and what you can do to break it as well as how to customize a general addiction cycle to fit your problem and help you overcome it.

Why the Addiction Cycle Is so Insidious

So, why is the addiction cycle so difficult to break? The answer is both extremely complex and very simple. The reason that the addiction cycle is so unmanageable is that it self-perpetuates. What that means is, the end of the cycle gets the beginning of the cycle going again – and this can go over and over and over until a huge outside force comes in and breaks it. In substance abuse and alcoholism treatment, they call this "hitting the bottom" or "getting sick and tired of being sick and tired." Let's go over the addiction cycle step-by-step.

The Emotional Trigger

The addiction cycle starts when you have that emotional trigger that makes you want to drink or smoke or shoot up or even go shopping or gamble. It is that emotional problem discussed in the last chapter that starts the cycle.

The Craving

The next stage in the cycle is craving. When you have your emotional moment it triggers the craving. For example, if a person experiences a problem in their life, they will use that addictive substance to cope with the problem. An addict will use their addictive substance both to cope with tragedy and to celebrate happy circumstances.

The Ritual

From there, a person will fall right back into the same addictive pattern – they will begin their old behaviours and associate with their old friends and fall right back into the cycle.

Reinforcing the Behavior

When they begin using it once again, they will be reinforcing that behaviour. Each time they go around the cycle it is going to reinforce their addiction a little bit more and eventually, they will begin to feel guilty and go on to the next stage of the cycle.

The Guilt

When someone feels guilty about their behaviour, and about the fact that they are using once again, the solution to coping with that guilt seems to be to continue using, which puts them right back into that addictive cycle from which it is so difficult to escape.

CHAPTER THREE

Why People Fail at Overcoming Addiction

In the last chapter, we discussed the addiction cycle and how getting trapped in it sort of feels like a fly that is caught between two panes of glass with no way out. This is one of the major reasons that people fail at overcoming their addiction, but it is by far not the only reason. In this chapter, we will explore some of the ways that people place destructive roadblocks in their way to prevent them from escaping their addiction.

Back to the Cycle

Most of the time, the reason that people fail at overcoming addiction is that every time they come to the end of their cycle it starts over again. It's like driving along the highway from one side of the country to the other, and desperately needing to stop and use the restroom but you cannot find a single exit ramp. The cycle of addiction – and the way it traps people – is the main reason that people fail at overcoming their addiction. But it is by no means the only reason.

They Don't Want to Quit

One reason that people fail to overcome their addiction is that they don't want to quit. In other words, they haven't reached that rock-bottom point that we discussed earlier. Any experience substance abuse counsellor will tell you that until someone hits rock bottom there is no chance of helping them. Of course, this is quite a common reason that people don't want to quit – they know that the drug or other substance is affecting their life, but they haven't seen major destruction yet and they are enjoying the feeling that they get from it. This is how every addiction on earth begins.

They Have a Destructive Environment

One of the reasons that people fail at overcoming their addiction is that the environment around them – which they have built during their addiction – is so destructive to getting clean or sober that they simply don't have the willpower to resist.

They Don't Have Any Help

Another problem is that people don't seek out help from those who can assist. For example, they don't seek out a substance abuse counsellor, they don't ask their family members to support them as they try to get clean and they don't have any friends that are not also addicts.

The Physical Withdrawal Symptoms Are Impossible to Endure

In rare cases, the physical withdrawal symptoms from a drug may be impossible to endure. For example, coming off heroin can be an extremely painful process that should be supervised by a medical professional. There are treatment centres that can help with withdrawal symptoms in drug protocols like methadone.

CHAPTER FOUR

Make a Commitment to Quit

The previous chapters of this book have dealt with understanding what addiction is rather than how to overcome it. That's because you need a solid understanding of how addiction works before you can start the process of treatment. This chapter will be the first in a step-by-step series on how to overcome your addiction.

Define Your Commitment

Before you make a commitment, you first need to figure out what commitment means to you. It is very easy to say to yourself that you will make a commitment to quit if what you are saying is that you will give it another try, even though you don't expect it to work. This is where a lot of people run into a problem with their commitment. They are making a commitment in the sense that is intended. What you need to do is make a commitment where you promise yourself you are going to do everything in your power to quit, without fail, without excuses and without the rationalizations that have caused you to start again in the past.

Set a Future Date

The object here is to set a date in the future when you're going to quit. Don't make that date tomorrow. Make that date have a significance of some kind. For example, if your birthday is coming up next month, that would be a perfect time to quit. Picking an arbitrary time to quit doesn't signify that you're committed. If you choose a day that means something, it is going to be harder to justify starting again with the idea of setting a new date in the future.

Tell Everyone

If you are planning to quit on a certain day then you should make it an event, and you should reinforce the fact that you won't be able to avoid quitting on that day by telling friends and family members who support you in overcoming your addiction that you plan on quitting on that particular day and remind them as it gets closer if you have said it for a future time that is way down the road.

Make Your Commitment Count

If your commitment doesn't mean anything to you then you are going to have no problem breaking it but if you make certain rules – such as giving yourself rewards after you have been able to achieve certain goals with your commitment, or giving yourself punishments for failing – then you might be able to have more success because your commitment will have strings attached to it that will make it much harder to ignore.

CHAPTER FIVE

The Pros and Cons of Addiction

In this chapter, we are going to evaluate the benefits and the detriments of your addictive behaviour. You need to know exactly what your substance is doing to your life that is causing you to want to quit. You also need to know how few the benefits are. You might think that you already know this, but putting it down on paper has real power, and seeing the pros and cons side-by-side can have a major impact. So, grab a piece of paper and a pen, or open up your smartphone or tablet and begin making a list.

The Pros

So, in this exercise, you are going to sit down for about 15 minutes and carefully think about exactly what benefits your substance offers you. If you write that there are no benefits then you have failed. If there were no benefits, you wouldn't keep doing it and so you need to be honest with yourself and write down the things that the substance does for you.

For example, a smoker can claim that smoking relieves their stress. Of course, that stress is usually caused by the withdrawal from nicotine in the first place, but smoking does lower stress levels. Think carefully and write down as many 'benefits' as you can.

The Cons

Now you are going to sit down and spend about the same amount of time coming up with the negative things that your addiction is bringing you. This will probably be a bigger list than your pros list by a whole lot. Of course, that's the goal of this exercise.

But don't put down things that aren't true because it just tells your subconscious mind that you're not taking it seriously and you're not planning on quitting when you come to your quit date and that it's perfectly acceptable to start using again whenever you choose. Write down all of the negative things that you can think of and then look at the two lists side-by-side.

Put Them Up Somewhere

Now, print them out if you can, or write them on a piece of paper if you can't and post them somewhere that you're going to see them every single day. You need to remind yourself constantly that there are almost no benefits to using your particular substance of choice and that there are lots and lots of good things about quitting.

On hard days, it is going to be worth having something on your wall that constantly reminds you of why you are quitting in the first place. Don't take these lists down until you get to the point where you're not thinking about your addiction every day.

CHAPTER SIX

Identify Your Triggers

In the previous chapter, we mentioned triggers; but unless you have been to *Alcoholics Anonymous* or received substance abuse treatment you might not understand exactly what your triggers are. This is one of the first steps to overcoming your addiction. A trigger is defined as an environment, behaviour, person, or thing that makes you want to partake in your substance of choice. Triggers can be extremely difficult to overcome and people that are used to giving in to every one of them and have multiple triggers throughout the day are going to have the hardest time giving up their addiction.

Some Examples of Triggers

There are so many examples of triggers out there that it is difficult to come up with examples that will be representative of all. Here are just a few from different addictions:

- A smoker who is triggered by a break at work because they always used to go out and smoke with their friends during their break.

- An alcoholic who has a hard time watching football because every time watched a football game in the past two years they were drunk – or well on their way.

- A drug addict who cannot pass a certain part of town because it is the same part of town where they used to get their drugs.

- Someone addicted to shopping who receives a new credit card offer in the mail and has to cut it in half as quickly as possible before it triggers a shopping trip.

- An overeater who sees an advertisement for their favourite pizza place, which is having an amazing deal on their favourite pizza, and they must deal with the craving that comes from that trigger.

How to Identify Your Triggers

Your next task is going to be to sit down and identify your triggers. You need to know what situations, people or things are going to make you want to use your particular substance of choice again. If you don't know what your triggers are, and you don't have a plan for dealing with them you are going to have a much smaller chance of overcoming your addiction because you are not avoiding the triggers or dealing with them as is necessary to overcome them.

You probably know some of the situations that trigger your use but you may not know all of them. It is rare for someone to know all of them the first time that they make their list. That's why you are giving yourself plenty of time to quit so that you can figure out what your triggers are long before the time comes when you are going to have to start overcoming them to beat your addiction.

Make a Quitting Plan

In this chapter, we are going to discuss how to make a quitting plan. You've completed the first two steps on your journey to recovery – making a commitment to quit, with a date to quit, and identifying your triggers. Now, you need to make a plan to avoid those triggers. Trying to quit without having a solid plan in place is like trying to bake a cake by reaching into the refrigerator and grabbing the first few ingredients you find and then mixing them in a big bowl. You aren't going to end up with any sort of cake that you'll want to eat unless you get incredibly lucky – like win-the-lottery-five-times-in-a-row lucky.

When to Make the Quitting Plan

In the last chapter, we discussed your triggers and how you could identify them. Now, you need to make a plan to deal with them. You want to create your quitting plan fairly close to the day that you're going to quit – within a week if possible. The reason for this is that first, things might change between now and then if you make a quitting plan right now and it may be obsolete by the time you get to your quitting day. Secondly, you are going to need to know what your triggers are – all of your triggers – before you can make a quitting plan.

How to Make the Quitting Plan

So, your quitting plan is going to consist of three parts. First, you are going to list the reasons why you are quitting. On your quit date, and every day afterwards, you are going to look at this list of reasons why you quit so they will be fresh in your mind throughout the entire day.

The second part of your quitting plan is a list of all of the triggers that you have identified and how you're going to deal with them. For example, if you are a smoker and talking on the telephone triggers your smoking habit, then get something to replace the cigarette that you would normally smoke while you were talking on the phone. Make sure that all of the triggers that are listed on your sheet – which you should have been writing down between the time you began and the quit date – have a plan in place for when you experience them because if not, the trigger could lead to your using it.

The third part of your plan is going to be your progress, which we are going to discuss in a later chapter. At the beginning of the day, you are going to review the reasons why you quit; you are going to have a plan in place for all the triggers that you have identified and at the end of each day, you are going to look over your progress and see how far you've come, to reinforce the fact that you have come too far to go back.

CHAPTER EIGHT

Prepare Your Environment

If you have a plan in place to overcome your triggers and you have done everything that has been recommended up until this point, your next step is going to be to prepare your environment. There are many things that you can do to prepare your environment but you are going to need to know what your triggers are before you can complete this step so you may want to wait until you are close to your quitting date. It will be almost impossible to do this step unless you wait until close to the day before your quit date.

Step One: Remove All Your Paraphernalia

So, the first step in preparing your environment is going to be removing all the paraphernalia that comes with using whatever particular substance that you use. If shopping is your addiction then you are going to remove your credit cards by cutting them up. If cigarettes are your addiction, you are going to throw away any cigarettes you have left, all of your lighters and all of the ashtrays that you have in your house. If you use alcohol or drugs then obviously you're going to want to get rid of the drugs and any needles or bongs or whatever you used to take the drug. The same goes with alcohol – get rid of everything in the house that could be considered alcoholic.

Step Two: Remove All of Your Trigger Objects

The next thing that you're going to do is remove all of the trigger objects that you have. This can be anything and it's going to be different for just about everyone. For example, there may be a certain chair that you always used in your house to take drugs, drink alcohol or smoke cigarettes. If this chair is going to remind you of your habit and it is going to trigger a craving then you need to get rid of it. Sometimes, all you have to do is move it to a different location or cover it with something (in the case of a chair), but other items will be more difficult.

Step Three: Change Your Habits

The next thing that you're going to have to do is change your habits – at least the ones that cause you to think about using your drug of choice for behaviour again. To use the example of shopping once again, you may have to stop going to the stores you once used. If you are addicted to drugs you may have to avoid the part of town where your drug hook-up usually hangs out. Whatever habits you have that might cause you to fail at your attempt to overcome your addiction – change them.

CHAPTER NINE

Seek Professional Help

One of the things to consider as you are making a plan is to seek professional help if you have access. Luckily, with the *Affordable Care Act*, many people have access to mental health evaluation and treatment that they probably never had before. This means that they can talk to someone about any mental health concerns that they have – and often can get treatment for conditions that have been causing them to "self-medicate" for a long time. For example, depression often masquerades as other problems and people use drugs or alcohol to help deal with their depressive states when all they could need is actual medication for depression or counsel.

Where to Find Professional Help

Finding professional help isn't all that difficult. You probably have several mental health places at your disposal – or the very least one – if you live in a city. If you live in more rural areas, then you may have to travel and one of the solutions that some people use is finding a therapist or mental health professional that they can communicate online. This is not ideal as they will usually not be able to prescribe medications if you need them, but it is an option if you must use them.

How to Use Professional Help

You'll probably be guided through the intake process of whatever mental health facility you decide to go to and they will probably have a plan in place for you. Generally, people that are getting treatment for mental health issues will see a therapist or counsellor and discuss issues or anything that is going on in their life and then will see a prescriber who will put them on medication if necessary. Then, you may be asked to attend certain classes, depending on your particular issue and the frequency with which you see your mental health provider will vary based on your treatment plan.

The Stigma Attached to Mental Health Issues

There are going to be many of you who are hesitant about seeing a mental health provider. After all, you are not crazy, right? There is a stigma attached to mental health issues and there really shouldn't be. You do not hide the fact that you take medication for diabetes or gout as prescribed by your doctor, so why are you ashamed of going to a mental health provider?

Even if this analogy doesn't convince you that mental health issues are nothing to be ashamed of, be aware that providers of mental health care are very discreet and there is little chance of anyone finding out that you are being seen by a therapist or taking medication for depression or another mental illness.

Surround Yourself with Support

The type of support mentioned in Chapter 9 is not the only kind of support that you want to have available to you as you begin this journey to overcome your addiction. You are going to need to make sure that you have people around you that will support you and help you on your road to success. This may mean getting rid of friends and loved ones, at least figuratively, and only associating with people who are supporting your decision to overcome your addiction. This is going to be a difficult process so here are some tips.

Explain Things without Making Personal Attacks

If you have people in your life that are standing in the way of your success then you need to sit down and explain to them that you aren't going to be able to associate with them anymore and why. But you must understand that you want to explain to these people why you're doing what you're doing without making any sort of judgment or personal attack. These can be other friends that you have with the same addiction as you or can even be a significant other, and while leaving someone is a difficult decision, it might have to be done if that person is going to make it impossible for you to quit.

Find Friends Who Can Support You

One of the things that you'll want to do is find friends who know what you are going through so that they can support you throughout your journey to overcome your addiction. *Alcoholics Anonymous* and *Narcotics Anonymous* are great resources for drug addictions and alcoholism as they are filled with people at varying levels of sobriety – with some of them having been sober for years. In larger cities, you're going to find all kinds of groups that can support just about every addiction you can imagine from gambling to overeating, from sex to pornography and everything in between. If you cannot find a support group within your area, then it is certain that there is going to be some type of forum or message board online for your particular addiction.

Family Members

One of the wildcards in the process of overcoming your addiction is going to be your family members. They say you can't choose your family and the adage is right but you can choose which family members you associate with the most. If you have family members who are not going to support you as you try to live without your addiction – especially someone who has a direct investment in you continuing to be addicted – you are going to need to avoid them at all costs.

CHAPTER ELEVEN

Handling Withdrawal Symptoms

In some cases, you are going to have to deal with withdrawal symptoms depending on what the addictive behaviour that you are trying to quit is. There are many ways to deal with withdrawal symptoms but it will all depend upon your treatment plan and what the particular thing is that you're trying to get off. We will go through the most common and how you can deal with the withdrawal symptoms of each.

Substance Abuse

Depending upon the drug that you are using, your withdrawal symptoms may be very mild or they may be extremely painful. In the cases where people have been addicted to drugs like methamphetamines or heroin for long periods – years even – treatment might have to be found at a facility that handles these types of withdrawal. With some drug withdrawals, if they are bad enough, death is a possibility so you want to make sure that you get help if you need it. As mentioned, some treatments for substance abuse can help you get through with the withdrawal symptoms without ending up with a further injury to your body or your mind. Methadone is one drug protocol that is used to get people off certain drugs and a plant called *kratom* is used in some countries.

Coming off Alcohol

If you are quitting drinking then you're going to experience anywhere from major to minor withdrawal symptoms depending upon how long you have been drinking and how regularly. Some of the withdrawal symptoms that come from getting off alcohol include irritability, headaches, nausea, shakes and possibly even hallucinations and seizures. If you have been drinking alcohol for a very long time it is dangerous to go through withdrawal symptoms without a qualified professional to oversee you.

Quitting Tobacco

If you are trying to quit tobacco products, nicotine is what is going to cause you withdrawal symptoms. Although nicotine withdrawal does not come with serious health risks, withdrawal from nicotine can still be troublesome. Often people gain a great deal of weight while they are quitting smoking because when you are craving nicotine one of the things that seem natural to do is to eat and continue snacking even if you're no longer hungry. To help combat withdrawal symptoms, solutions like nicotine patches, lozenges and other nicotine replacement products have been on the market for years.

Other Withdrawal Symptoms

As for the rest of the things that people get addicted to, you are mostly going to have mental withdrawal problems rather than physical ones. You may have to look up advice for your specific addiction to plan to combat it.

CHAPTER TWELVE

Celebrate Your Success

One of the things that people sometimes do when they are overcoming an addiction is to not hold their successes in high enough regard. There is no doubt in anyone's mind that overcoming an addiction is one of the most monumental things that you could accomplish. Unfortunately, this is not something that is going to endure for a while and then end, with you being addiction free for the rest of your life. This is something that you're going to be enduring for the rest of your life. That's why it is more important than ever to celebrate the successes that you have and the milestones that you have set for yourself.

Setting Milestones

One of the things that you're going to want to do is set milestones for yourself, which tell you how far you have come along your journey when you reach them. If we use tobacco as an example, a person might start with shorter distances and then expand them such as three days, two weeks, 30 days, six months, etc. That is based loosely on some of the addiction milestones for smokers such as how long until your body is free of nicotine. You will be setting your milestones for whatever addiction you have, and you will be creating a type of reward whenever you reach that milestone.

Setting up Rewards

It is important to note that when you set up your rewards you don't want to do anything that is going to put your newfound sobriety at risk. Whatever addictive behaviour you're trying to beat, you don't want your rewards to get you back into that habit. A perfect example of this happening is trying to overcome food addiction and set a reward for themselves – at a certain milestone – to go to an all-you-can-eat buffet and have as much as they want. The problem with this reward is that it triggers addictive behaviour. Doing that, for an overeater, is the equivalent of a heroin addict getting high because they reached six months without any heroin.

Celebrate Your Daily Success As Well

Remember, overcoming addiction is a process that happens one day at a time. That is a common phrase used in *Alcoholics Anonymous* – one day at a time. That means that every day that you can make it through without giving in to your previous addiction is a day worth celebrating. While you don't have to come up with a complicated reward for each day, you can pat yourself on the back and give yourself kudos for making it through another day without succumbing.

CHAPTER THIRTEEN

Track Your Progress

One of the things that you can do to help motivate yourself is to track your progress. That's why it was included in part of the plan that you will be following every day. This chapter is going to show you how to track your progress so that you can understand exactly how far you've come and use it in your plan of action to overcome addiction.

Your Daily Diary

One of the things that you're going to want to keep if you're trying to overcome addiction is a daily diary that allows you to put down exactly how you felt that day and how you overcame it. This is also a great way to externalize some of the frustration they are going to be feeling from coming off of whatever addiction you're trying to stop. Keeping a diary or journal of your progress allows you to read it when you're feeling you're most vulnerable and see what kind of things you did the last time you are feeling this way to overcome it. The Journal also helps you to see how far you have come. If you look back over six months of diary entries, you will think twice about giving in to your addictive behaviour.

32 Days Without an Accident

Have you seen those signs that sometimes hang in industrial warehouses and factories where they list how many days they've gone without an accident? This is meant to encourage employees to be safer so that they can get that number as high as possible – that's the theory anyway. You are going to do the same thing with your number of days. Post a whiteboard or something else on the wall that you can change easily to show how many days you have gone without giving in to your addiction. This will motivate you to keep going and lift you up when you feel as if you are going to give in.

Track Your Progress Periodically

When it comes to some addictive behaviour, you're going to want to track your progress periodically as well. For example, if you are trying to lose weight by overcoming an eating addiction then you may want to keep track of your current weight and the weight loss that you have achieved up until this point. There may be other addictions as well that would benefit from tracking progress periodically.